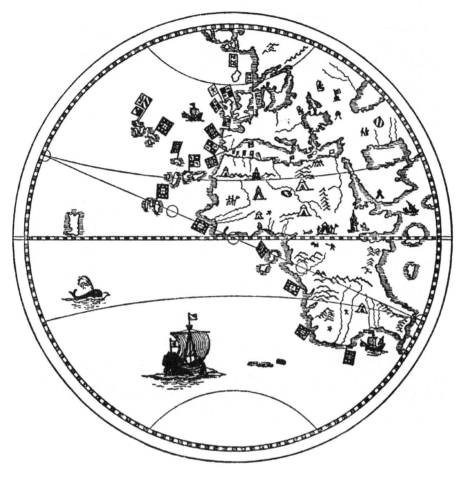

MARTIN BEHAIM'S GLOBE

The LOG of CHRISTOPHER COLUMBUS' first VOYAGE to AMERICA in the year 1492

as copied out in brief by BARTHOLOMEW LAS CASAS, one of his companions,

with illustrations by J. O'H. COSGRAVE, II   London: W.H.ALLEN & CO.LTD.

Martino Publishing
Mansfield Centre, CT
2011

LONGWOOD PUBLIC LIBRARY

Martino Publishing
P.O. Box 373,
Mansfield Centre, CT 06250 USA

ISBN 1-891396-91-9

© *2011 Martino Publishing*

All rights reserved. No new contribution to this publication may
be reproduced, stored in a retrieval system, or transmitted, in any form or
by any means, electronic, mechanical, photocopying, recording, or otherwise,
without the prior permission of the Publisher.

Cover design by T. Matarazzo

Printed in the United States of America On 100% Acid-Free Paper

De Insulis inuentis

Epistola Cristoferi Colom (cui etas noſtra
multū debet : de Inſulis in mari Indico nup
inuētis. Ad quas perquirendas octauo antea
menſe:auſpicijs et ere Inuictiſſimi Fernandi
Hiſpaniarum Regis miſſus fuerat)ad Mag⸗
nificum dīm Raphaelez Sanxis:eiuſdē ſere⸗
niſſimi Regis Theſaurariū miſſa. quam nobi
lis ac litteratꝰ vir Aliander ð Coſco: ab Hiſ⸗
pano ydeomate in latinū conuertit:tercio kl̄s
Maij. M.cccc.xciij. Pontificatus Alexandri
Sexti Anno Primo .

Q Uoniam ſuſceptē ꝓuintie rem ꝑ⸗
fectam me ꝓſecutum fuiſſe:gratū ti
bi foꝛe ſcio:has ꝑſtitui exarare:que
te vniuſcuiuſꝗ rei in hoc noſtro iti⸗
nere geſte inuēteꝗ admoneāt. Triceſimoter
tio die poſtꝗ Gadibus diſceſſi:in mare Indi⸗
cū perueni:vbi plurimas Inſulas innumeris
habitatas hominibꝰ repperi:quaꝝ oīm ꝓ feli
ciſſimo Rege noſtro:pꝛeconio celebꝛato ꞇ ve
xillis extenſis:cōtradicente nemine poſſeſſio
nē āccepi.primeꝗ earum:diui Saluatoꝛis no
men impoſui (cuius fretꝰ auxilio) tam ad hāc
ꝗ ad ceteras alias ꝑuenimꝰ. Eain vero Indi

Regnū hyspanie.

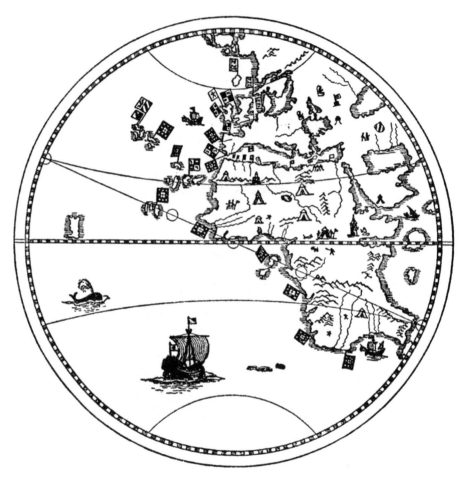

MARTIN BEHAIM'S GLOBE

The LOG *of* CHRISTOPHER COLUMBUS'
as copied out in brief by BARTHOLOMEW LAS CASAS, *one of his companions,*

MADE IN THE YEAR 1490

---

first VOYAGE *to* AMERICA *in the year 1492*

with illustrations by J. O'H. COSGRAVE, II.   *London:* W.H. ALLEN & CO. LTD.

Venient annis
Secula seris, quibus Oceanus
Vincula rerum laxet, et ingens
Pateat tellus, Tiphisque novos
Detegat orbes, nec sit Terris
Ultima Thule

*In the last days there will come
an age in which Ocean shall loosen
the bonds of things; a great country
will be discovered; another Tiphis
shall make known new worlds, and
Thule shall no longer be the extremity
of the earth.*

—SENECA: *Chorus to Medea*
[*first century before Christ*]

EVIDENCES OF LAND
IN THE WEST

Martin Vincent, Pilot of the King of Portugal, relates that 450 leagues West of Cape St. Vincent, he picked up a log curiously carved, but not with iron, which had been brought there by a westerly wind.

Another carved fragment of wood which came from the West had been seen near Porto Santo by Pedro Correa, brother-in-law of Columbus.

Others reported "reeds of such bigness that a single joint would contain nine garrafas of wine." No such reeds grew in western Europe or Africa.

The inhabitants of the Azores related to Columbus that after a course of westerly winds the sea cast up pine trees which were not the growth of those parts, and at another time the sea brought the bodies of two men of strange race to the island of Flores. Still another time covered boats, or almadias, had been cast up on the shore.

HERE BEGIN
THE WORDS OF
CHRISTOPHER COLUMBUS,
HIGH ADMIRAL OF THE OCEAN SEA,
ADDRESSED TO KING FERDINAND
AND QUEEN ISABELLA

In the Name of Our Lord

JESUS CHRIST

Whereas, *Most Christian, High, Excellent and Powerful Princes, King and Queen of the Spains and of the Islands of the Sea, Our Sovereigns, in this year of Grace, 1492, after Your Highnesses had overthrown the powers of the Moors at the City of Granada, where in this present year on the second day of January, I saw the royal banners of your majesties planted by force of arms upon the battlements of the Alhambra, which is the fortress of that city, and saw the Moorish King come forth from the gates of the city and kiss the royal hands of Your Highnesses, and of my Lord the Prince; and in the present month, in consequence of the information which I had given Your Highnesses concerning the lands of India, ruled by a prince called the Grand Can, which in our language means King of Kings, and how he and his ancestors had often sent to Rome for learned men who might instruct him in our Holy Faith, and how the Holy Father had never complied, so that many believing in idolatry were lost to the doctrines of perdition; therefore, Your Highnesses, as Catholic Christians and defenders of the Christian Faith against the doctrines of Mohamet and all other idolatries, did* resolve to **send me**, Christopher Columbus, to these parts of India and to this prince and his people to learn their disposition and the proper means of converting them to the Christian Faith; and ordered that I should not go to the eastward as is customary, but by a westerly route, in which direction we have hitherto no certain evidences that anyone has gone.

Thus, after expelling the Jews from your domains in the same month of January, Your Highnesses ordered that I should go with sufficient fleet to this same part of India, and for that purpose most graciously elevated me to the title of Don, High Admiral of the Sea and perpetual Viceroy and Governor of all islands and continents that I should discover and gain both now and hereafter in the Ocean Sea, and that my son should succeed me and so on from generation to generation forever.

Hereupon, I left the city of Granada on Saturday, May 12, 1492, and came to the town of Palos which is a seaport, where I did arm three vessels for such enterprises; and departed from that port well supplied with provisions and with many sailors, on the 3rd day of August of the same year, being Friday, half an hour before sunrise. I steered for the Canary Islands of Your Highnesses, which are in the said Ocean Sea, that I might thence set out for the Indies to perform the embassy to the princes there, so as to comply with my orders. As *part of my duty, I thought it well to write an account of all the voyage most punctually, noting the happenings from day to day, as will hereafter appear. Moreover, I did resolve to describe each night what had passed in the day and to note each day how I had navigated at night. I intend to draw up a nautical chart which shall contain the several parts of the ocean and land in their proper situation; and also to compose a book to represent the whole by pictures with latitudes and longitudes, on which accounts it behooves me to abstain from my sleep and make many trials in navigation, which will demand much labor.*

HERE BEGINS THE LOG OF
CHRISTOPHER COLUMBUS'
FIRST VOYAGE TO AMERICA,
AS COPIED OUT IN BRIEF
BY ONE OF HIS
COMPANIONS

SET SAIL from the bar of Saltes at eight o'clock *Friday* and sailed with a strong sea breeze till sunset *August 3, 1492* towards the south for fifteen leagues. Afterwards steered S. W. and S. by W., which is the direction of the Canaries.

Saturday
August 4, 1492

Steered S. E. by S.

FIRST VOYAGE TO AMERICA

Sailed day and night more than forty leagues.

Sunday
August 5, 1492

Monday
August 6, 1492 The rudder of the caravel Pinta became unshipped making the steering most difficult. It was suspected that this had been planned by Gomez Rascon and Christopher Quintero, to whom the caravel belonged, for they dreaded to go on the voyage. The Admiral says that before setting out these men had been inclined to oppose and "pull holes," as they say. The Admiral was much disturbed at not being able to help the Pinta without danger, but he says he was somewhat quieted when he thought how brave and energetic a man was Martin Alonzo Pinzon, Captain of the Pinta. Made during the day and night twenty-nine leagues.

The Pinta's rudder again broke loose. Secured it, and made for the island of Lanzarote, one of the Canaries. Sailed, day and night, twenty-five leagues.

Tuesday
August 7, 1492

Wednesday
August 8, 1492
There were differing opinions among the pilots of the three vessels as to their true situation, but that of the Admiral proved to be nearer the truth. He was anxious to go to Grand Canary in order to leave the caravel Pinta there, since she was steering badly and making water, and he wished to secure another vessel if one were to be found. They were unable to reach the island that day.

FIRST VOYAGE TO AMERICA

The Admiral was not able to reach the island of *Thursday* Gomera till Sunday night. Because the Pinta could *August 9, 1492* not be navigated, Martin Alonzo remained at Grand Canary by command of the Admiral.

HERE THE VOYAGE IS INTERRUPTED
WHILE THE PINTA IS
REPAIRED

The Admiral returned to Grand Canary and there with great labor and the help of Martin Alonzo and the others repaired the Pinta. Rigged her with square sails instead of the lateen sails that she had carried before. Finally sailed to Gomera.

Saw great flames of fire burst from a high mountain on the island of Teneriffe.

Saturday
September 1, 1492

Three days
September 2–4, 1492

Returned to Gomera with the Pinta repaired. The Admiral says that many honorable Spanish gentlemen, inhabitants of the island of Hierro, declared that every year they saw land to the west of the Canaries. And others, natives of Gomera, confirmed the same on oath. The Admiral here says that he remembers, while he was in Portugal in the year 1484, that a man came to the King from the island of Madeira to beg for a caravel to search out this land that was seen. This man swore that it could be seen every year and always in the same way The Admiral also says that he remembers that the same lands of the same shape and size and in the same direction had been seen by the inhabitants of the Azores.

After taking in wood, water, meat, and other provisions which had been provided by the men left on
shore when he went to Grand Canary to repair the
Pinta, the Admiral was now ready to start on the
long voyage with the three vessels.

Wednesday
September 5, 1492

HERE BEGINS THE LONG VOYAGE
INTO UNCHARTED
WATERS

SET SAIL from the harbor of Gomera this morn- *Thursday*
ing and shaped the course for the voyage. The *September 6, 1492*
Admiral learned by a vessel from the island of Hierro
that there were three Portuguese caravels cruising
about with the object of taking him—this must have
been the result of the King of Portugal's envy that
Columbus should have gone to Castile to the King
and Queen of Spain. It was calm the whole day and
night.

Friday
September 7, 1492 In the morning were between Gomera and Teneriffe. All Friday and Saturday until three o'clock at
night, becalmed.

FIRST VOYAGE TO AMERICA

Three o'clock at night it began to blow from the *Saturday*
N. E. Shaped the course to the West. Shipped much *September 8, 1492*
sea over the bows which made progress slow. Day
and night went nine leagues.

Sunday
September 9, 1492   Sailed this day nineteen leagues, and determined to count less than the true number, that the crew might not be dismayed if the voyage should prove long. In the night sailed thirty leagues at the rate of ten miles an hour. The sailors steered badly, letting her fall away to the N. E. even to half a point; concerning this the Admiral many times rebuked them.

This day and night sailed sixty leagues at the rate of *Monday* ten miles an hour. Reckoned only forty-eight leagues, *September 10, 1492* that the men might not be terrified if they should be long upon their voyage.

Tuesday
September 11, 1492

Steered a course W. and sailed above twenty leagues. Saw a large fragment of the mast of a vessel, apparently of a hundred and twenty tons, but could not pick it up. In the night sailed about twenty leagues, and reckoned only sixteen, for the reason already given.

This day steered the same course. Sailed day and *Wednesday*
night thirty-three leagues, and reckoned less for the *September 12, 1492*
same reason.

Thursday
September 13, 1492
This day and night sailed W. thirty-three leagues against the currents. Reckoned three or four less. On this day, at the commencement of the night, the needles turned a half point to north-west, and in the morning they turned somewhat more north-west.

Steered this day and night W. twenty leagues; reckoned somewhat less. The crew of the Nina reported that they had seen a tern and a boatswain bird, or water-wagtail. These birds never go farther than twenty-five leagues from the land.

Friday
September 14, 1492

Saturday
September 15, 1492

Sailed day and night W. twenty-seven leagues and more. In the beginning of the night saw a marvellous bolt of fire fall from the heavens into the sea at a distance of four or five leagues.

Sailed day and night W. thirty-nine leagues and reckoned only thirty-six. Some clouds and small rain. The Admiral says that on that day and ever afterwards they met with very temperate breezes so that there was great pleasure in enjoying the mornings. These were most delightful, wanting nothing but the melody of the nightingales. He compares the weather to that of Andalusia in April. Began to meet with large patches of weeds, very green, which appeared to have been recently washed away from land. From this judged some island was near, though not a continent according to the opinion of the Admiral, who says, *the continent we shall find further ahead.*

Sunday
September 16, 1492

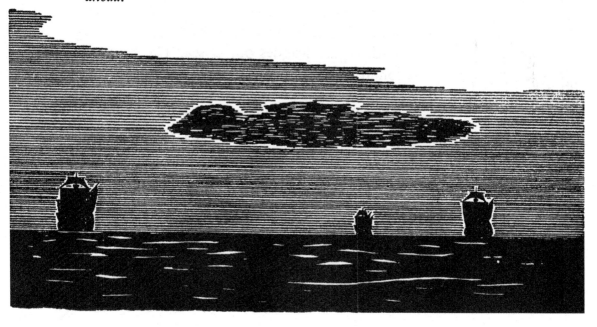

Monday
September 17, 1492
Steered W. and sailed, day and night, above fifty leagues; wrote down only forty-seven. Current favorable. Saw a great deal of weed which proved to be rock-weed. It came from the W. and was met with very frequently. Were of opinion that land was near. The pilots took the sun's amplitude and found that the needles declined N. W. a full quarter. The seamen were terrified and dismayed without saying why. The Admiral discovered the cause, and ordered them to take the amplitude again the next morning, when they found that the needles were true. The cause was that the star moved from its place, while the needles remained stationary. At dawn saw many more weeds, apparently river weeds, and among them a live crab which the Admiral kept. He said that these are sure signs of land, never being met with eighty leagues out at sea. The sea-water was found to be less salt than it had been since leaving the Canaries. The breezes were always soft. All very cheerful. Strove which vessel should outsail the others and be the first to discover land. Saw many

tuna fish and the crew of the Nina killed one. The Admiral here says that these signs of land came from the West, *in which direction, I trust in that high God in whose hands are all victories, we very soon shall sight land.* This morning he saw a white bird called a water-wagtail which has not the habit of sleeping on the sea.

Monday Continued

Tuesday
September 18, 1492
This day and night made more than fifty-five leagues; wrote down only forty-eight. All this time the sea was very smooth and the ships sailed upon it as they would have done upon the river at Seville. This day Martin Alonzo with the Pinta, which was a swift sailer, ran ahead of the other vessels. He called to the Admiral from his caravel that he had seen great flocks of birds flying westward and that he expected to see land that night. For this reason he pressed onward. A great mass of dark, heavy clouds appeared in the north, which is a sign of being near the land.

Continued on, and sailed, day and night, twenty-five leagues, experiencing a calm. Wrote down twenty-two leagues. On this day at ten o'clock a booby came to the ship, and in the afternoon another arrived. These birds do not generally venture more than twenty leagues from the land. It drizzled without wind, which is a sure sign of land. The Admiral did not wish to cause delay by beating to the windward in search of land, although he held it for certain that there were islands to the north and south. This in fact was the case, for he was sailing in the midst of them. His wish was to sail on to the Indies, since there was such fair weather. *For if it please God,* as the Admiral says, *we shall examine these parts upon our return.* Here the pilots found their places upon the charts. The reckoning of the Nina made her 440 leagues distant from the Canaries, that of the Pinta 420, that of the Admiral 400.

Wednesday
September 19, 1492

Thursday
September 20, 1492 Steered W. by N., varying with alternate changes of wind and calm. Made seven or eight leagues' progress. Two boobies came on board, and afterwards another, a sign of the nearness of land. Saw large quantities of weeds today, though none were seen yesterday. Caught a bird with the hand which is like a tern. It was a river bird and not a sea bird, with feet like those of a gull. At dawn three land birds came singing to the ship. They disappeared before sunset. Afterwards saw a booby coming from W. N. W. and flying to the S. W., an evidence of land to the westward. These birds sleep on shore and go to sea in the morning in search of food, never flying more than twenty leagues from land.

Most of the day calm, afterwards a little wind. *Friday*
Steered the course day and night, sailing less than *September 21, 1492*
thirteen leagues. At dawn saw so much weed that
the ocean seemed to be covered with it. The weed
came from the West. Saw a booby. The sea smooth
as a river, and the finest air in the world. Saw a whale, a
sign of land, as they always keep near the coast.

Saturday
September 22, 1492

Steered about W. N. W., her head turning from one point to another, varying the course and making about thirty leagues. Saw few weeds. Some sand-pipers were seen and another bird. The Admiral here says, *this head wind was very necessary to me, for my crew had grown much alarmed at the thought that in these seas no wind ever blew in the direction of Spain.* Part of the day saw no weeds. Later they were very thick.

Sailed N. W. and N. W. by N. and at times W. *Sunday*
nearly twenty-two leagues. Saw a turtle dove, a *September 23, 1492*
booby, a river bird, and other white fowl. There
was a great deal of weed with crabs in it. The sea being smooth and tranquil, the sailors murmured, saying that they had got into smooth water, where the
wind would never blow to carry them back to Spain.
Afterwards the sea rose without wind, which aston-
ished them. The Admiral says on this occasion, *the
rising of the sea was very favorable to me, such as had
only happened before in the time of the Jews when they
went out of Egypt and murmured against Moses, who
delivered them out of captivity*

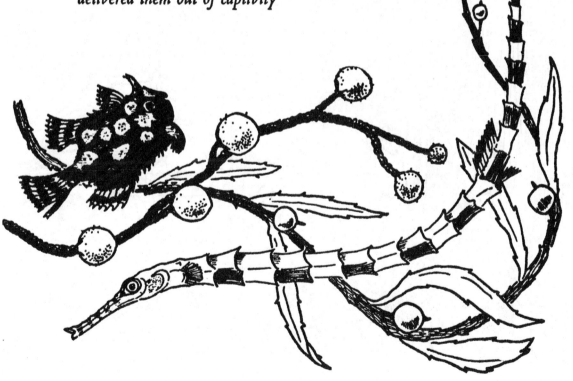

Monday   Continued the course W. and sailed, day and night,
September 24, 1492   fourteen leagues and a half; reckoned twelve. A
booby came to the ship. Saw many sandpipers.

This day began with a calm and afterwards the wind rose. Continued the course W. till night. The Admiral held a conversation with Martin Alonzo Pinzon, captain of the Pinta, respecting a chart which the Admiral had sent him three days before. On this chart it appears he had marked down certain islands in the sea. Martin Alonzo said that the ships were in the position on which the islands were placed. The Admiral replied that so it appeared to him, but it might be that they had not fallen in with them owing to the currents which had always carried the ships to the N. E. and that they had not made as much progress as the pilots stated. The Admiral then asked for the chart to be returned to him, and it was sent back on a line. Then he began to plot their positions upon it in the presence of the pilot and sailors.

Tuesday
September 25, 1492

At sunset Martin Alonzo went up on the poop of his ship and called out with great joy from his vessel to the Admiral, claiming the reward as he had sighted land. The Admiral says that when he heard this he fell on his knees and returned thanks to God, and

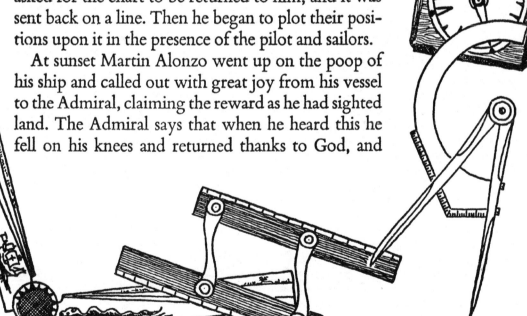

Tuesday Continued Martin Alonzo with his crew repeated *Gloria in excelsis deo,* as did the crew of the Admiral. Those on board the Nina ascended the rigging, and all declared they saw land. The Admiral also thought it was land, and about twenty-five leagues distant. They remained all night repeating these affirmations, and the Admiral ordered their course to be shifted from W. to S. W. where the land appeared to lie. They sailed that day four leagues and a half W., and in the night seventeen leagues S. W.; in all twenty-one and a half. Told the crew thirteen leagues, making it a point to keep them from knowing how far they had sailed. For it was always feigned to them that all the distances were less, so that the voyage might not appear so long. Thus two reckonings were kept, the shorter being feigned and the longer being the true one. The sea very smooth. Many of the sailors went in it to bathe alongside the ships. Saw many dories, or dolphins, and other fish.

Continued the course W. till the afternoon, then S. W. and discovered that what had been taken for land was nothing but clouds. Sailed, day and night, thirty-one leagues; reckoned to the crew twenty-four. The sea was like a river, the air sweet and very soft.

Wednesday
September 26, 1492

Thursday
September 27, 1492   Continued the course W. and sailed, day and night, twenty-four leagues. Reckoned to the crew twenty. Saw many dolphins and killed one. Saw a tropic bird.

Continued the course W. and sailed day and night with calms, fourteen leagues. Reckoned thirteen. Met with little weed. Caught two dolphins, the other vessels more.

Friday
September 28, 1492

Saturday
September 29, 1492

Continued the course W. and sailed twenty-four leagues; reckoned to the crew twenty-one. On account of calms made little progress this day. Saw a bird called a *Rabihorcado*, or man-of-war bird, which forces the boobies to disgorge what they have swallowed, and then eats it. This is its only way of getting food. It is a sea bird, but does not sleep on the sea and does not go more than twenty leagues from land. There are many of them in the Cape Verde Islands. Afterwards there came two boobies. The air was soft and refreshing, and the Admiral says nothing was wanting but the singing of the nightingale. The sea smooth as a river. Three times saw boobies, and a *Rabihorcado*. Many weeds appeared.

Continued W. and sailed, day and night in calms, *Sunday*
fourteen leagues. Reckoned eleven. Four boatswain *September 30, 1492*
birds came to the ship, which is a very clear sign of
land, for so many birds of this kind together is a sign
that they are not straying or lost. Twice saw boobies.
Many weeds. Note that when night falls the stars
called The Guardians are near the arm on the West
side, and when dawn breaks are on the line below
the arm to the N. E., so that it seems in the
whole night they move only three lines, which are
nine hours. This is the case every night. Moreover
at nightfall the needles decline a quarter N. E., and
at dawn they are true with the star. From this it
appears that the star moves and the needles always
point true.

Monday
October 1, 1492
Continued the course W. and sailed twenty-five leagues. Reckoned to the crew twenty. There was a heavy shower. At dawn the Admiral's pilot made the distance from Hierro 578 leagues to the West. The short reckoning which the Admiral showed his crew gave 584, but the true one which the Admiral calculated and kept secret was 707.

Continued W., day and night, thirty-nine leagues. *Tuesday*
Reckoned to the crew thirty. The sea always smooth. *October 2, 1492*
Many thanks be to God, says the Admiral here. Weeds
came from the E. towards the W., contrary to their
usual course. Saw many fish and took one. A white
bird, which appeared to be a gull, was seen.

Wednesday
October 3, 1492

Continued the usual course, and sailed forty-seven leagues. Reckoned to the crew forty. Many sandpipers seen, and great quantities of weed, some of it old, and some very fresh, which appeared to contain fruit. Saw no other birds. The Admiral believed the islands plotted on his chart had been passed. The Admiral here says that he did not wish to keep the ships beating up and down as they had the week before, when there were so many signs of land. Though he knew there were islands in that quarter, his wish was to proceed onward to the Indies. To linger on the way he thought would not be wise.

Continued the course W. Sailed, day and night, sixty-three leagues and reckoned to the crew forty-six. There came to the ship more than forty sandpipers in a flock, with two boobies. A ship's boy on board the caravel hit one of them with a stone. There also came a man-of-war bird to the ship, and a white bird like a gull.

Thursday October 4, 1492

Friday
October 5, 1492 Continued on the course and sailed eleven miles an hour; day and night, fifty-seven leagues. Reckoned to the crew forty-five. The wind abated in the night. Fine weather and the sea smooth. *To God*, says the Admiral, *be many thanks given*. The air soft and temperate, with no weed, many sandpipers, and flying-fish coming on the deck in numbers.

The Admiral continued his course and sailed forty *Saturday*
leagues, day and night. Reckoned to the crew thirty- *October 6, 1492*
three. This night Martin Alonzo Pinzon said that
they had better steer from W. to S. W. The Admiral
thought from this that Martin Alonzo did not wish
to proceed onward to Japan. But he considered it
best to keep his course, as he should probably reach
the land sooner in that direction, preferring to visit
the continent first and then the islands.

Sunday
October 7, 1492
Continued W. and sailed twelve miles an hour for two hours, then eight miles an hour. Sailed, till an hour after sunrise, twenty-three leagues. Reckoned to the crew eighteen. All the vessels were striving to outsail one another and gain the reward promised by the King and Queen by first discovering land. At sunrise the caravel Nina, which kept ahead on account of her swiftness in sailing, hoisted a flag on her masthead, and fired a lombard as a signal that she had discovered land, for such was the Admiral's order. He had also ordered that at sunrise and sunset the ships should join him, as the air was more favorable at those times for seeing the greatest distance, the haze clearing away. Towards evening seeing no land, and observing large flocks of birds coming from the N. and making for the S. W., the Admiral determined to alter his course. He thought it probable that the birds were either going to the land to pass the night or abandoning the countries of the North, flying from the winter. Knowing that the Portuguese had discovered most of the islands they

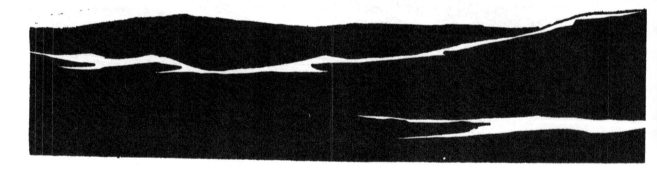

possessed by following the flight of birds, the Admiral shifted his course from W. to W. S. W. with a resolution to continue two days in that direction. This was done about an hour after sunset. Sailed in the night nearly five leagues, and twenty-three in the day. In all twenty-eight.

Sunday Continued

Monday
October 8, 1492

Steered W. S. W. and sailed, day and night, eleven or twelve leagues; at times during the night, fifteen miles an hour. Found the sea like the river at Seville, *thanks to God,* says the Admiral. The air soft as that of Seville in April, and so fragrant that it is delicious to breathe it. The weeds seemed very fresh. Many land birds. Took one that was flying towards the S. W. Also terns, ducks, and a pelican were seen.

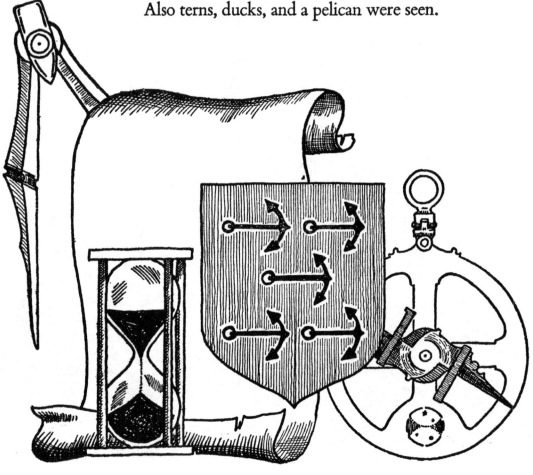

Sailed S. W. five leagues, when the wind changed, and then stood W. by N. four leagues. Sailed in the whole day and night twenty leagues and a half. Reckoned to the crew seventeen. All night heard birds passing.

Tuesday
October 9, 1492

Wednesday
October 10, 1492

Steered W. S. W. and sailed at times ten miles an hour, at others twelve, and at others, seven. Day and night, made fifty-nine leagues' progress. Reckoned to the crew but forty-four. Here the men could bear no more and complained of the length of the voyage. But the Admiral encouraged them in the best way he could, giving them good hope of the advantages they might gain from it. He added that however much they might complain, having come so far, he had nothing to do but go to the Indies, and he would go on until he found them, with the help of our Lord.

Steered W. S. W. There was a heavier sea than had *Thursday*
been met with before in the whole voyage. Saw *October 11, 1492*
sandpipers and a green rush near the vessel. The
crew of the Pinta saw a cane and a log. They also
picked up a stick which appeared to have been carved
with an iron, a piece of cane, a plant which grows on
land, and a board. The crew of the Nina saw other
signs of land and a stalk loaded with roseberries.
Everyone breathed afresh and rejoiced at these signs.
Sailed this day till sunset, twenty-seven leagues.

After sunset steered their original course W. and
sailed twelve miles an hour till two hours after mid-
night, going twenty-two leagues and a half. As the
Pinta was the swiftest sailer and kept ahead of the
Admiral, she discovered land and made the signals
ordered by the Admiral. The land was first seen by a
sailor called Rodrigo de Triana, although the Admiral at ten o'clock that evening, being on the castle
of the poop, saw a light, but so small a body that he
could not affirm it to be land. Calling to Pero Gu-
tierrez, gentleman of the King's bedchamber, he

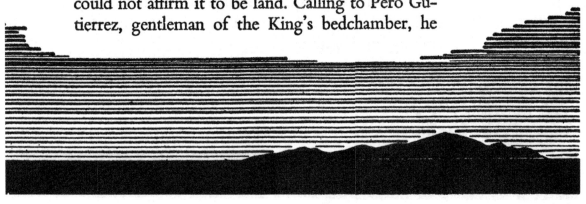

Thursday
Continued told him he saw light and bid him look that way, which he did and saw it. The Admiral said the same to Rodrigo Sanchez of Segovia, whom the King and Queen had sent with the fleet as inspector, but he could see nothing, because he was not in a place whence anything could be seen. After the Admiral had spoken he saw the light once or twice again, appearing and disappearing like the light of a wax candle moving up and down. Few thought this an indication of land, but the Admiral held it for certain that land was near. For which reason, after they had said the *Salve* which the seamen are accustomed to repeat and chant after their fashion, the Admiral directed them to keep a strict watch upon the forecastle and to watch well for land. To him who should first cry out that he saw land he said he would give a silken doublet besides the reward of 10,000 maradevis a year which the King and Queen had offered. At two o'clock in the morning the land was sighted at the distance of two leagues. Shortened sail, remaining under the square-sail, and the vessels were hove to, waiting for daylight.

When it grew light they found themselves near a small island, one of the Lucayos, called in the Indian language *Guanahani*. Presently they saw people, naked, and the Admiral went on shore in the armed boat, along with Martin Alonzo Pinzon, and Vincent Yanez, his brother, Captain of the Nina. The Admiral bore the royal standard, and the two captains each carried a banner of the Green Cross, which all the ships had carried. This contained the initials of the names of the King and Queen each side of the cross, and a crown over each letter. Arrived on shore, they saw trees very green, many streams of water, and fruits of many kinds. The Admiral called to the two captains, and to others who leaped on shore, and to Rodrigo de Escovedo, secretary of the whole fleet, and to Rodrigo Sanchez, of Segovia, to bear witness that before all others he took possession (as in fact he now did) of that island for the King and

Friday
October 12, 1492

Queen, his sovereigns, making the declarations that are required, as is most largely set down in testimonies which were then made in writing. Presently large numbers of the inhabitants crowded to the shores. Here follow the actual words of the Admiral:

As I saw that they were very friendly to us and perceived that they could be much more easily converted to our holy faith by gentle means than by force, I presented them with some red caps, and strings of glass beads to put round their necks, and many other trifles of small value, which gave them great pleasure. Wherewith they were much delighted, and this made them so much our friends that it was a marvel to see. Afterwards they came swimming to the boats, bringing parrots, balls of cotton thread, javelins, and many other things which they exchanged for articles we gave them, such as glass beads and Hawks' bells. In fine, they took all and gave what they had with good will. But they seemed on the whole to me to be a very poor people. They all go as naked as when their mothers bore them, even the women, though I saw but one girl. All

whom I saw were young, not above thirty years of age, well made, with fine shapes and faces. Their hair is short, and coarse like that of a horse's tail. They wear the hairs brought down to the eyebrows combed towards the forehead, except a few locks behind, which they wear long and never cut. Some paint themselves black, some paint themselves white, others red, and others with such colors as they can find. Some paint the face, and some the whole body, others only around the eyes, and others the nose. They are like the Canarians, neither black nor white. Weapons they have none, nor are acquainted with them, for I showed them swords, which they grasped by the blades and cut themselves through ignorance. They have no iron, their darts being wands without iron and nothing more than sticks. Some of them have a fish's tooth at the end, others being pointed in various ways. The people are all of a good size and stature, with good faces and well made. I saw some with scars of wounds upon their bodies, and asked by signs the cause of them. They answered me in the same way that there came people from other islands in the neighborhood with the intention of seizing them,

*Friday
Continued*

*Friday
Continued* *and they defended themselves. I thought then, and still be-
lieve, that these came from the mainland to take them
prisoners. It appears to me that the people are ingenious
and would be good servants, and I am of opinion that they
would very readily become Christians, as they appear to
have no religion. They very quickly learn such words as
are spoken to them. If it please our Lord, I intend at my
return to carry home six of them to your Highnesses, that
they may learn our language. I saw no beasts on this
island of any kind, except parrots.*

These are the words of the Admiral.

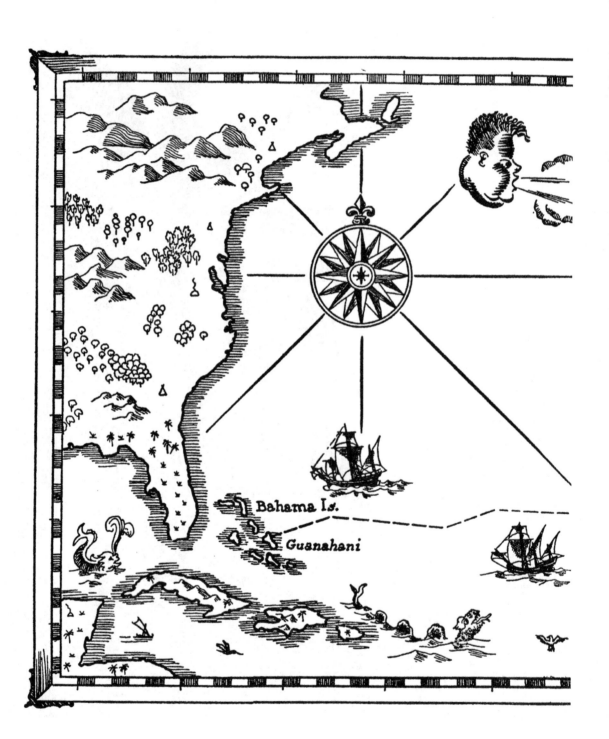

Bahama Is.

Guanahani

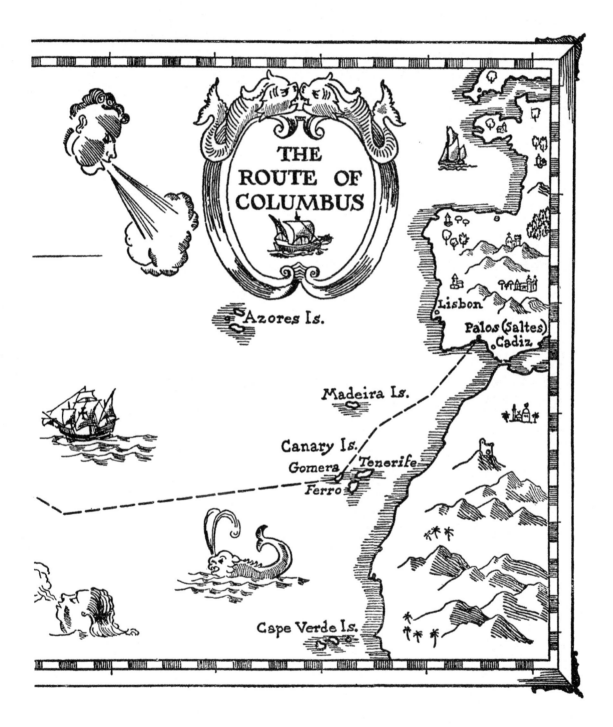

THE
ROUTE OF
COLUMBUS

Azores Is.

Lisbon

Palos (Saltes)
Cadiz

Madeira Is.

Canary Is.
Gomera   Tenerife
Ferro

Cape Verde Is.

HERE BEGINS AN ACCOUNT OF
THE FIRST TWO DAYS IN AMERICA
TOGETHER WITH WOODCUTS FROM
THE LETTER OF COLUMBUS
PUBLISHED UPON HIS
RETURN

Saturday, October 13, 1492

At daybreak great multitudes of men came to the shore, all young and of fine shapes, and very handsome. Their hair was not curly but loose and coarse like horse-hair. All have foreheads much broader than any people I had hitherto seen. Their eyes are large and very beautiful. They are not black, but the color of the inhabitants of the Canaries. Nor should anything else be expected, they being in the same latitude with the island of Hierro in the Canaries. They are straight limbed without prominent bellies, and are very well formed. They came to the ships in small canoes made of a single trunk of a tree wrought in a wonderful manner considering the country. Some of them are large enough to contain forty or forty-five men, others smaller, and some only large enough to hold one man. They rowed with an oar like a baker's shovel, and go at a marvellous rate. If they happen to upset, they all jump into the sea, and swim till they have righted their canoe and bailed it out with the calabashes that they carry with them. They came loaded with balls of cotton, parrots, javelins, and other things too numerous to mention. These they exchanged for whatever we chose to give them. I was very attentive to them, and strove to learn if they had any gold. Seeing some of them with little bits of metal hanging at their noses, I gathered from them by signs that by going southward or steering round the island in that direction, there would be

found a king who possessed great cups full of gold, and in large quantities. I tried to get them to go there but found they were unacquainted with the route. I determined to stay here till the evening of the next day, and then sail for the S.E.; for, according to what I could learn from them, there was land at the S. and N.W. as well as at the S.W. The natives from these lands came many times and fought with them, and proceeded on to the S.W. in search of gold and precious stones. This island is rather large and very flat, with bright green trees and a very large lake in the center without any mountain. The whole land is so green that it is a pleasure to look on. The natives are very docile, and desirous to possess anything they saw with us. But not having anything to give in return, they take what they can get and presently swim away. Still they give away all they have got for whatever may be given to them, down to broken bits of crockery and glass. I saw one give sixteen skeins of cotton thread which weighed above twenty-five pounds for three Portuguese ceutis, the skeins being as much as an arroba of cotton thread. This traffic I forbade, and suffered no one to take their cotton from them, unless I should order it to be procured for your Highnesses, if proper quantities could be met with. It grows in this island, but from my short stay here I could not satisfy myself fully concerning it. The gold, also, which they wear in their noses, is found here, but not to lose time, I am determined to see if I can find the island of Japan. Now, as it is night, all the natives have gone on shore with their canoes.

Sunday, October 14, 1492

At dawn I ordered the ship's boat and the boats of the caravel to be got ready and coasted along the island toward the N.N.E. to see the other side of it, we having landed first on the eastern side. Presently I saw two or three villages, and the people all came down to the shore, calling out to us, and giving thanks to God. Some brought us water, and others food; others seeing that I was not disposed to land, plunged into the sea and swam out to us. We understood that they asked us if we had come from heaven. One old man came on board my boat. The others, both men and women cried with loud voices, "Come and see the men who have come from heaven. Bring them food and drink." There came many of both sexes, everyone bringing something, giving thanks to God, throwing themselves on the ground, and lifting up their hands to heaven. They shouted to us to come on shore, but I was afraid to land, seeing an extensive reef of rocks which surrounds the whole island. Although within there is a depth of water and room sufficient for all the ships of Christendom, there is a very narrow entrance. There are some shoals withinside, but the sea has no more motion than the water in a well. In order to see all this I set out in the morning, for I wished to give a full account to your Highnesses, as also to find out where a fort might be built. I discovered a tongue of land which appeared like an island, though it was not one, but might

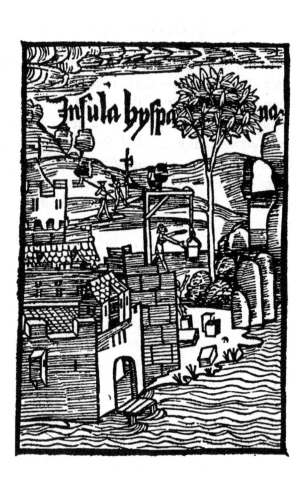

be cut through and made so in two days. On it were six houses. I do not, however, see the necessity of thus fortifying the place, as the people here are simple in war-like matters, as your Highnesses will see by those seven which I caused to be taken and carried to Spain in order to learn our language, and return, unless your Highnesses should order them all to be brought to Castile, or to be kept as captives on the same island. I could conquer the whole of them with fifty men and govern them as I pleased. Near the islet I have mentioned were groves of trees, the most beautiful I have ever seen, with leaves as green as those of Castile in the month of April and May. There were also many streams. After having taken a survey of these parts, I returned to the ship, and set sail. I saw so many islands that I knew not which first to visit. Those natives whom I had taken on board informed me by signs that there were so many of them that they could not be numbered; they repeated the names of more than a hundred. I determined to steer for the largest, and so I did. It will be distant about five leagues from San Salvador; and the others, some more, and some less. All are very flat, and all are inhabited. The natives make war on each other, although these are very simple-minded and handsomely formed people.

These are the words of the Admiral

peragant solennia sacra. festacp fronde velent
delubra. Exultet Christ'i terris: queadmodu
in celis exultat: cum tot populorum pditas asi
hac animas saluatum iri preuidet. Letemur z
nos: tu ppter exaltratione nostre fidei. tum p=
pter reru temporaliu incremeta: quoz no solu
Hispania sed vniuersa Christianitas est futu=
ra priceps. Hec vt gesta sunt sic breuiter enar=
rata. Uale. Ulisbone pridie ydus Marcij.

Cristofor' Colom Occane classis Prefect'.

Epigrama. R. L. de Corbaria Episcopi
Montispalusij
Ad Inuictissimu Rege Hispaniaz

Jam nulla Hispanis tellus addenda triuphies
Atcp parum tantis virib'/orbis erat.
Nunc longe Eois regio deprensa sub vndis.
Auctura est titulos Betice magne tuos.
Unde repertori merito referenda Colubo
Gratia: sz summo est maior habenda deo:
Qui vinceda parat noua regna tibicp sibicp
Tecp simul fortem prestat z esse pium.

Fernãdº rex hyspania

WITHDRAWN

$8.50

LONGWOOD PUBLIC LIBRARY
800 Middle Country Road
Middle Island, NY 11953
(631) 924-6400
longwoodlibrary.org

LIBRARY HOURS

Monday-Friday	9:30 a.m. - 9:00 p.m.
Saturday	9:30 a.m. - 5:00 p.m.
Sunday (Sept-June)	1:00 p.m. - 5:00 p.m.

CPSIA information can be obtained
at www.ICGtesting.com
Printed in the USA
BVOW09s2149070917
494270BV00004B/43/